A Kalmus Classic Edition

Ferdinand
SIEBER

36 EIGHT-MEASURE VOCALISES
FOR ELEMENTARY VOCAL TEACHING

Opus 93

FOR MEZZO-SOPRANO

K 09183

Elementary Vocalises
for
Mezzo - Soprano.

FERD. SIEBER. Op. **93**.

N. B. All the exercises are to be sung, at first, on various vowels (a, o, e), and, later, on the syllables written underthem. Do *not* observe, at first, the directions given for shading, but execute each exercise in a quiet, smooth *piano*, and as *legato* as possible. The tempo to be employed depends on the needs and the ability of the singer. At every rest, and at the breathing-marks (✛), breath *must* be taken; it *may* also be taken (if necessary) at the commas (,).

4

9183

9183

9

9183

10

9183

14

9183

9183

9183

18

9183